Simple
Clean Keto

REALISTIC LOW CARB
RECIPES

PAULA KISH

Forward

I can't believe the day to publish this has finally come. So much emotion, excitement and love went into this cookbook. I'm so full of joy for Paula to be published and shared in a way to help people and bring God the glory. In here are several of my favorite dinner recipes that I like and hope you will too. We love how people can take our ideas and customize them to each one's liking. Enjoy ~~ Ed Kish

TABLE of CONTENTS

CHAPTER 1
APPETIZERS & SNACKS

"I know once people get connected to real food, they never change back"

Taco Meatballs

PREP TIME: 10 MIN   COOK TIME: 20   SERVINGS: 12 Meatballs

INGREDIENTS

- 1 lb ground beef
- 1 egg
- 2 Tbsp taco seasoning (pg 21)
- 3 colby jack snack cheese sticks cut into 12 cubes

Serving Size: One Meatball
Nutrition:
Carbs 1g
Protein 9g
Fat 8g
Calories 111

METHOD

Mix ground beef, egg and my homemade taco seasoning together in a bowl. Separate into 12 equal pieces. Flatten each piece into a flat circle. Place a piece of cheese into the circle and surround cheese with beef until it is completely enclosed in a ball. Do this until you have 12 cheese filled meatballs. Place onto a baking sheet. Bake in a 375 degree oven for 20 minutes or until cooked through. Serve with salsa and sour cream.

These can be stored in the refrigerator for up to five days and frozen for up to two months.

4

Bacon Knots

PREP TIME: 10 MIN   COOK TIME: 15 MIN   SERVINGS: 12 Knots

INGREDIENTS

- 12 slices bacon
- 1 tsp Italian seasoning
- 1/4 cup grated parmesan cheese

Serving Size: One Knot
Nutrition:
Carbs 0g
Protein 3g
Fat 3g
Calories 37

METHOD

Pre-heat oven to 375 degrees. Tie each piece of bacon into a loose double knot. Place knots onto a baking sheet. Sprinkle Italian seasoning & Parmesan cheese onto each bacon knot. Place baking sheet into oven for 12-15 minutes or until desired doneness.

These can be stored in the refrigerator for up to five days.

NOTE: These are also delicious if you leave the seasoning off and after baking dip them into melted chocolate.

Cheesy Sausage Balls

PREP TIME: 10 MIN   COOK TIME: 20 MIN   SERVINGS: 12 Meatballs

INGREDIENTS

- 1 lb breakfast sausage
- 1/2 cup pork rind crumbs
- 8 oz cream cheese, softened
- 1 cup shredded cheddar cheese

Serving Size: One Sausage ball
Nutrition:
Carbs 1g
Protein 11g
Fat 24g
Calories 259

METHOD

Preheat the oven to 375. degrees. Add all of the ingredients into a mixing bowl and combine it all together. Roll the mixture into 12 balls.
Place the sausages balls on a parchment lined baking sheet and bake for 20 minutes until lightly browned and cooked through.

These can be stored in the refrigerator for up to five days and frozen for two months.

Air Fried Pickles

PREP TIME: 10 MIN   COOK TIME: 12 MIN   SERVINGS: 4

INGREDIENTS

- 20 dill pickle chips
- 1/2 cup crushed pork rinds
- 1/2 cup grated parmesan cheese
- 2 beaten eggs
- 1 tsp seasoned salt

Serving Size: 5 Pickles
Nutrition:
Carbs 3g
Protein 12g
Fat 9g
Calories 140

METHOD

Start by drying pickles on a paper towel.
Mix pork rind crumbs, parmesan cheese and seasoning together in a bowl. Dip pickles, one at a time into the egg, then coat with crumbs. Place in air fryer and set temperature at 375 degrees for 10-12 minutes or until golden brown and crisp. Serve with Ranch or Sugar Free Ketchup.

Jalapeño Poppers

PREP TIME: 20 MIN   COOK TIME: 15 MIN   SERVINGS: 12

INGREDIENTS

- 6 Jalapeño peppers
- 4 oz softened cream cheese
- 1 tsp garlic powder
- 1/2 cup shredded cheddar cheese
- 1/2 tsp smoked salt
- 1/4 cup bacon crumbles

Serving Size: One Popper
Nutrition:
Carbs 2g
Protein 3g
Fat 9g
Calories 95

METHOD

Slice peppers in half and carefully scoop out seeds and dispose. Mix cream cheese, garlic powder and 1/2 of the shredded cheese together in a small bowl, then fill the peppers with the cream cheese mixture. Top with remaining cheese and bacon pieces.

Once they are all filled, place them in an oven preheated at 400. Bake for about 12-15 minutes or until cheese is brown and bubbly.
I prefer to use my air fryer. They come out nice and crispy. 400 degrees for 13-15 minutes.

These can be stored in the refrigerator for up to five days and frozen for two to three months.

Crab Stuffed Deviled Eggs

PREP TIME: 20 MIN   SERVINGS: 12

INGREDIENTS

- 6 hard-boiled eggs, peeled and sliced in half
- lengthwise 1 tsp Old Bay
- seasoning
- 1/4 cup mayonnaise
- 1 tsp dijon mustard
- 5 ounces crabmeat, drained
  1 tsp dried parsley

Serving Size: One Half Egg
Nutrition:
Carbs 0g
Protein 5g
Fat 6g
Calories 81

METHOD

Cut each egg in half and scoop out the yolks. Mix the egg yolks with seasoning, mayonnaise, mustard and crabmeat in a small bowl. Fill each egg white with about a teaspoon scoop of egg yolk mixture. Sprinkle a light dusting of Old Bay seasoning onto each egg. Garnish with dried parsley.

Store in refrigerator in an airtight container for up to four days.

Cloud Bread

PREP TIME: 5 MIN   COOK TIME: 25 MIN   SERVINGS: 8

INGREDIENTS

- 4 eggs, yolks & whites separated Into two bowls
- 4 oz softened cream cheese

Serving Size: one piece
Nutrition:
Carbs 1g
Protein 4g
Fat 8g
Calories 88

METHOD

Beat egg whites until stiff peaks form. Add cream cheese to egg yolks and mix with mixer until well blended. Fold egg whites into yolk mixture until blended. You can add desired seasonings or keep them plain.

Line baking sheet with parchment paper. Drop big spoonfuls of batter onto parchment, leaving space in between. They will be flat similar to pita bread.

Bake in preheated oven at 300 degrees for 25 minutes.

Let cool and store in refrigerator.

This is a very delicate, melt in your mouth bread.

Refrigerate for up to five days. Freeze for up to two months.

Fat Head Pizza Dough

PREP TIME: 10 MIN   COOK TIME: 25 MIN   SERVINGS: 10

INGREDIENTS

- 1-1/4 Cup Mozzarella Cheese
- 6 oz Cream Cheese
- 3/4 Cup Almond Flour
- 2 Eggs
- 1 tsp garlic powder (optional)

Serving Size: one slice of 10
Nutrition:
Carbs 4g
Fiber 1g
Protein 8g
Fat 13g
Calories 156

METHOD

Melt 2 Cheeses together in microwave for 2 minutes. Stir in the rest of the ingredients and press out to desired thickness between parchment paper that has been sprayed with nonstick spray on both sides that will be in contact with the dough. Bake crust at 400 degrees for 8 minutes. Dough will not be fully baked, just firmed up. Add desired toppings and finish baking in oven 10-15 minutes.

You can get creative with this dough and make things like, bread sticks, meat pie crust, bagels, rolls etc.
This dough can be frozen for two months.

CHAPTER 2
SOUP & SALAD

"Small changes usually add up to huge results"

Chicken & Broccoli Cheese Soup

PREP TIME: 10 MIN   COOK TIME: 20 MIN   SERVINGS: 6

INGREDIENTS

- 4 Tbsp butter
- 1/2 cup diced onion
- 1 tsp salt
- 1/2 tsp pepper
- 1 tsp minced garlic
- 32 oz chicken broth
- 1 large bunch of broccoli cut into bite size pieces, including stalk
- 4 oz cream cheese cubed
- 8-oz cheddar cheese
- 1/2 tsp xanthan gum
- 1 cup shredded cooked chicken

METHOD

Sauté onion and Broccoli stalk in butter for a few minutes, add garlic, salt & pepper. Sauté until onions are translucent. Add chicken broth and remainder of broccoli pieces. Once it starts boiling, reduce heat and simmer covered with lid for about 10 minutes or until broccoli is fork tender. Add cream cheese, cheddar cheese and chicken. Sprinkle xanthan gum across the top. The xanthan gum acts as a thickener. Stir until melted and thick. Refrigerate for up to three days.

Serving Size: one cup
Nutrition:
Carbs 7g
Fiber 1g
Protein 21g
Fat 27g
Calories 352

Chicken Tortilla Soup

PREP TIME: 10 MIN   COOK TIME: 30 MIN   SERVINGS: 8

INGREDIENTS

- 1 Tbsp olive oil
- 1/2 cup diced onions
- 2 garlic cloves, minced
- 1/2 tsp Salt
- 2 cups cooked shredded chicken
- 2 tsp chili powder
- 1 tsp dried oregano
- 28 oz diced tomatoes
- 2 cups chicken broth
- 1- 4 oz can diced green chilies
- 1/8 cup cilantro chopped

METHOD

Sauté onions for about 5 minutes. Add garlic and saute another 2 minutes. Add remaining ingredients and simmer about 20-30 minutes. Top with extra cheese and sour cream. Store in refrigerator for up to three days.

Serving Size: one cup
Nutrition:
Carbs 7g
Fiber 2g
Protein 28g
Fat 5g
Calories 195

Creamy Tomato Soup

PREP TIME: 5 MIN   COOK TIME: 15 MIN   SERVINGS: 4

INGREDIENTS

- 24 oz low carb marinara
- sauce 10 oz chicken broth
- 1/4 Cup heavy cream

Serving Size: one cup
Nutrition:
Carbs 8g
Fiber 1g
Protein 5g
Fat 14g
Calories 167

METHOD

Heat sauce and broth in sauce pan on the stovetop until hot and bubbly. Add heavy cream at the end and heat through. If you desire a smoother tomato soup, use an immersion blender to blend soup before serving. Store in refrigerator for up to three days.

Paula's Signature Chili

SERVINGS: 12

PREP TIME: 15   PREP TIME: 45

INGREDIENTS

- 2 lbs ground beef
- 1/2 cup diced onion
- 4 Tbsp chili powder
- 2 tsp garlic powder
- 2 tsp onion powder
- 1 tsp salt
- 2 tsp paprika
- 2 tsp cumin
- 1 tsp oregano
- 1/2 tsp pepper
- 28 oz can crushed tomatoes
- 1 can Rotel tomatoes
- 2 cups beef broth

METHOD

Saute onions for a couple of minutes then add ground beef and brown. Drain fat. Add all of spices and stir into beef. Add liquid and tomatoes and simmer for about 20-30 minutes. Store in refrigerator for up to three days. Freeze for up to two months.

Serving Size: one cup

Nutrition:

Carbs 8g

Fiber 3g

Protein 22g

Fat 13g

Calories 240

Broccoli Salad

PREP TIME: 20   SERVINGS: 6

INGREDIENTS

- 5 cups fresh broccoli chopped into bite sized pieces
- 1/2 cup cooked bacon crumbles
- 1/4 cup red onion diced
- 1 Tbsp sunflower seeds
- 1/2 cup shredded cheddar cheese 3/4 Cup mayonnaise
- 1 Tbsp apple cider vinegar
- 1 Tbsp granular Monkfruit or Stevia
- 1/2 tsp Salt

METHOD

Place first five ingredients into a large serving bowl. Mix last four ingredients in a small bowl then pour over broccoli mixture and mix well. Refrigerate until ready to serve. Store in refrigerator for up to three days.

Serving Size: one cup
Nutrition:
Carbs 7g
Fiber 2g
Protein 6g
Fat 26g
Calories 280

17

Caesar Salad

PREP TIME: 15   SERVINGS: 2

INGREDIENTS

- One whole head or heart of Romaine lettuce
- 1/4 cup shredded Parmesan cheese
- Caesar Dressing (recipe pg 25)

Serving Size:
one cup salad with dressing
Nutrition:
Carbs 3g
Fiber 2g
Protein 11g
Fat 28g
Calories 304

METHOD

Chop Romaine into bite size pieces. Add desired amount of Caesar dressing and toss to coat all of the lettuce. Sprinkle cheese on top and toss again.

Note: I use a wooden salad bowl. I like to take a fresh, peeled garlic clove and rub it on the inside of the bowl, drizzle a small amount of olive oil and salt as I am working it in. It really takes the flavor up a notch!

Bacon & Egg Salad

PREP TIME: 15   SERVINGS: 2

INGREDIENTS

- 3 boiled eggs
- 1/2 cup mayonnaise
- 1 tsp Dijon mustard
- 1/2 tsp salt
- 1/4 tsp pepper
- 2 slices cooked chopped bacon

METHOD

Peel and rough chop eggs in a bowl. Add mayo, mustard, salt, pepper and chopped bacon. Stir until combined. Refrigerate for up to three days.

Serving Size: 1/2 of salad
Nutrition:
Carbs 1g
Fiber 0g
Protein 13g
Fat 56g
Calories 565

CHAPTER 3
CONDIMENTS

"Food is really and truly the most effective medicine"

Taco Seasoning

PREP TIME: 5 MIN   SERVINGS: 30

INGREDIENTS

- 6 tbsp chili powder
- 4 tsp ground cumin
- 3 tsp paprika
- 2 tsp garlic powder
- 2 tsp onion powder
- 1 tsp black pepper
- 1/8 - 1/4 tsp cayenne pepper
- 1 tsp salt

METHOD

Mix all ingredients together and store in an airtight container in the pantry for up to six months.

Serving Size: One tsp
Nutrition:
Carbs 1g
Fiber 1g
Calories 7

Creamy Avocado Mayonnaise

PREP TIME: 15 MIN   SERVINGS: 16

INGREDIENTS

- 1 egg yolk plus 1 yolk (Pasteurized eggs highly recommended)
- 1 tsp Dijon mustard
- 1 Tbsp white wine vinegar
- 1 cup avocado oil
- 1/2 tsp salt
- Pinch of pepper

Serving Size: One tbsp
Nutrition:
Carbs 0g
Protein 1g
Fat 14g
Calories 131

METHOD

Fill a tall glass jar with all of the ingredients. Use an immersion blender to blend the ingredients until thick and creamy. This Process takes about five minutes. It will also work in a blender but immersion is preferred.

Store in the refrigerator for up to four days.

Ranch Vegetable Dip

PREP TIME: 5 MIN   SERVINGS: 28

INGREDIENTS
- 1 cup sour cream
- 3/4 cup mayonnaise
- 2 oz cream cheese, softened
- 2 Tbsp dried Ranch seasoning

METHOD
Mix ingredients together and refrigerate for at least two hours before serving. Best served chilled. Great for veggies & dehydrated meat.

Store in the refrigerator for up to four days.

Serving Size: One Tbsp
Nutrition:
Carbs 1g
Protein 0g
Fat 7g
Calories 63

Fiesta Dip

PREP TIME: 5 MIN   SERVINGS: 28

INGREDIENTS

- 1 cup sour cream
- 1/2 cup mayonnaise
- 2 oz cream cheese, softened
- 10 oz Rotel original
- 2 Tbsp Ranch seasoning
- 1/2 cup Mexican blend cheese

Serving Size: One Tbsp
Nutrition:
Carbs 1g
Protein 1g
Fat 5g
Calories 50

METHOD

Mix ingredients together and refrigerate for at least two hours before serving. Best served chilled. Great for veggies & dehydrated meat.

Store in the refrigerator for up to four days.

Caesar Salad Dressing

PREP TIME: 5 MIN   SERVINGS: 30

INGREDIENTS

- 1 cup mayonnaise
- 1/4 cup grated parmesan
- cheese 2 garlic cloves minced
- 2 tbsp olive oil
- 2 tsp dijon mustard
- 2 tsp lemon juice
- 1 tsp Worcestershire sauce
- 1/2 tsp Salt
- 1/4 tsp pepper

METHOD

Mix all ingredients together. Serve over fresh romaine lettuce and top with shredded parmesan cheese.

Store in the refrigerator for up to five days.

Serving Size: One Tbsp
Nutrition:
Carbs 0g
Protein 0g
Fat 7g
Calories 62

Creator Unknown

Paula's Signature Coleslaw Dressing

PREP TIME: 5 MIN   SERVINGS: 28

INGREDIENTS

- 1 cup mayonnaise
- 4 tsp white vinegar
- ¼ cup Allulose sweetener
- 1 tsp Dijon mustard
- 1/2 teaspoon salt

METHOD

Mix all together and refrigerate for 30 minutes, serve. Store in a jar in the refrigerator and pour over coleslaw as needed.

Store in the refrigerator for up to five days.

Serving Size: One Tbsp
Nutrition:
Carbs 0g
Protein 0g
Fat 6g
Calories 54

Blue Cheese Dressing

PREP TIME: 5 MIN   SERVINGS: 28

INGREDIENTS

- 1/2 cup mayonnaise
- 1/2 cup sour cream
- 1/4 cup crumbled blue cheese
- 1 tablespoon heavy cream, more depending on the desired thickness
- 1 tsp lemon juice
- ½ teaspoon garlic powder
- ½ teaspoon salt

METHOD

Mix all together and refrigerate for 30 minutes, serve. Store in the refrigerator for up to five days.

Serving Size: One Tbsp
Nutrition:
Carbs 0g
Protein 1g
Fat 5g
Calories 45

CHAPTER 4
BREAKFAST

"Food is an important part of a balanced diet"

Baked French Eggs

PREP TIME: 10 MIN   COOK TIME: 20 MIN

INGREDIENTS

- eggs (One per egg cup)
- 1 tsp heavy whipping cream
- 1 Tbsp shredded Gouda Cheese
- Salt & Pepper to taste

Serving Size: One Egg Cup
Nutrition:
Carbs 1g
Protein 6g
Fat 4g
Calories 59

METHOD

Spray muffin tin with non-stick cooking spray. Crack one egg into each muffin tin, as many as you want to make. Do not break the egg yolk. Pour one tsp Heavy Cream onto each egg. Top with shredded cheese. I like Gouda with this recipe. Add salt and pepper if desired. Bake in preheated 375 degree oven for 18-22 minutes depending on how soft or firm you like your yolk. Once done, run a butter knife or thin spatula around the sides and pop them out.

These can be stored in the refrigerator in an airtight container for up to four days and can be frozen for two to three months.

Microwave for one minute to reheat.

Stuffed Waffles

PREP TIME: 10 MIN   COOK TIME: 10 MIN   SERVINGS: 2

INGREDIENTS

- 2 eggs
- 1 cup shredded mozzarella cheese
- 1 tsp vanilla extract
- 1/4 cup softened cream cheese
- 2 tsp granular Monkfruit or Stevia
- Berries (optional)
- Sugar free / low carb pancake syrup

METHOD

Preheat mini waffle iron. Mix eggs, cheese & vanilla extract in a small bowl. Spray non-stick spray onto waffle iron. Place two tablespoons of batter into the waffle iron. This recipe makes 4-6 waffles. Mix cream cheese together with sweetener. Once waffles are done, spread cream cheese mixture in between two waffles and top with fresh berries, if desired, butter and syrup.

Serving Size: two waffles with cream cheese not including berries and syrup.
Nutrition:
Carbs 4g
Protein 22g
Fat 26g
Calories 332

Chorizo Quiche

PREP TIME: 15 MIN   COOK TIME: 45 MIN   SERVINGS: 6

INGREDIENTS

Crust:
- 1-1/2 cups almond flour
- 1/4 cup melted butter
- 1/4 tsp salt
- 1 egg

Filling:
- 10 oz Chorizo
- 1/4 cup diced onion
- 6 eggs beaten
- 1/2 cup heavy cream
- 6 oz Pepper Jack cheese
- Salt & Ppper to taste

Serving one slice
Carbs 9g
Fiber 3g
Protein 23g
Fat 50g
Calories 566

METHOD

Mix all together and press into a 9" pie plate. Bake in a preheated 350 degree oven for 10 minutes. The crust will be partially baked. Remove from oven and prepare filling.

Sauté onions in butter, add chorizo and cook through. Add Chorizo & onions to partially baked pie crust. Pour cream into eggs and beat along with salt and pepper. Pour over chorizo then top with cheese. Bake at 350 degrees for 30-35 minutes. The edges should be firm and the center should be just a little bit jiggly.

Store in refrigerator for up to four days.

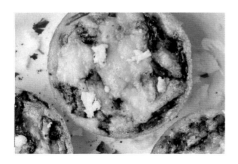

Spinach & Feta Egg Cups

PREP TIME: 10 MIN   COOK TIME: 20 MIN   SERVINGS: 6

INGREDIENTS

- 6 eggs
- 1 cup chopped fresh spinach
- 1/2 cup feta cheese
- 1 tsp salt
- 1/2 tsp pepper

Serving Size: One Egg Cup
Nutrition:
Carbs 1g
Protein 8g
Fat 8g
Calories 112

METHOD

Preheat oven to 375. Spray muffin tin with nonstick spray. Beat eggs in a small bowl. Add chopped spinach, feta, salt and pepper. Mix all together. Pour equal amounts into six muffin cups. Place on a baking sheet in case of overflow. Bake for 18-20 minutes or until eggs are springy when pressed on.

Store in the refrigerator for up to four days. Freeze for up to two months.

Reheat in microwave for one minute.

Pancakes

PREP TIME: 10 MIN   COOK TIME: 10 MIN   SERVINGS: 8-
                                                      10 Pancakes

INGREDIENTS

- 4 eggs
- 3 oz softened cream cheese
- 1/2 to 3/4 cup almond flour (depending on how thick or thin you want them)
- 1 tsp vanilla extract
- 1 tsp baking powder
- 1 tsp sweetener (optional)

METHOD

Mix all ingredients together in a blender or with an electric mixer. Pour onto heated skillet or griddle. Turn when batter is firmed up.

Store in refrigerator for up to five days or freeze for up to twp months.

Serving Size: One Pancake

Nutrition:

Carbs 2g

Fiber 1g

Protein 5g

Fat 10g

Calories 118

Sausage Gravy

PREP TIME: 5 MIN   COOK TIME: 20 MIN   SERVINGS: 4

INGREDIENTS

- 1 lb breakfast sausage 2
- Tbsp butter
- 1 tsp Xanthan gum
- 1 cup heavy cream
- 1 Cup Chicken Broth
- salt & pepper to taste

Serving Size: 1 Cup
Nutrition:
Carbs 4g
Fiber 0g
Protein 23g
Fat 58g
Calories 627

METHOD

Chop and Brown sausage in a skillet, add butter. Once sausage is brown, sprinkle xanthan gum over sausage. Stir a minute or two until the xanthan gum absorbs the butter and grease. Pour Heavy Cream over sausage and add salt and pepper. Stir until the gravy thickens. Add broth a little at a time until desired consistency is achieved, stirring often. This is great served over a chaffle or even on eggs.

Easy Crepes

PREP TIME: 5 MIN   COOK TIME: 10 MIN   SERVINGS: 2

INGREDIENTS

- 4 eggs
- 2 Tbsp heavy cream
- 1/2 tbsp salt
- 2 Tbsp gelatin
- 1 Tbsp powdered sweetener
- 1 tsp vanilla extract

Serving Size: 1 Crepe no filling
Nutrition:
Carbs 2g
Fiber 0g
Protein 24g
Fat 21g
Calories 302

METHOD

Place first 6 ingredients into a blender and blend on high for about 2 minutes.
Lightly, spray crepe pan with avocado oil spray. Make sure pan is hot. Swirl a thin layer of batter onto pan. Tilt pan to fill In holes. Spread with crepe spreader or spatula Flip once batter is dry. Crepe should be. lightly brown on both sides. Let cool, then add filling. I have an easy filling recipe below that I mix and put into an n2o whipped cream dispenser can.

Filling:
- 1 cup heavy cream
- 2 Tbsp Sweetener
- 1 tsp vanilla extract
- pinch of salt

Basic Chaffle

PREP TIME: 5 MIN   COOK TIME: 3-4 MIN   SERVINGS: 4

INGREDIENTS

- 2 eggs beaten
- 1 cup shredded mozzarella cheese

Serving Size: one chaffle
Nutrition:
Carbs 1g
Protein 10g
Fat 9g
Calories 119

METHOD

Mix eggs and cheese together in a small bowl. Spray a mini waffle iron with nonstick spray. Place two tablespoons of batter into the waffle iron at a time.

If you want your chaffles to be crispy, add a little extra cheese to the top and bottom side and cook until desired texture. Reheat in an air fryer, toaster or microwave.

Store in refrigerator for up to five days. Freeze for up to two months.

CHAPTER 5
DINNER

"Food is an important part of a balanced diet"

Paula's Signature Lasagna

PREP TIME: 10 MIN   COOK TIME: 45   SERVINGS: 6

INGREDIENTS

- 2-lbs ground beef
- 24 oz low carb pasta sauce
- 12 oz mozzarella cheese
- 4 Crepini egg wraps
- 1 tsp salt
- 1/2 tsp pepper
- 1 tsp dried basil

Serving Size: one piece
Carbs 7g
Fiber 1g
Protein 32g
Fat 30g
Calories 411

METHOD

Brown ground beef in a skillet and drain fat. Add salt, pepper & basil. In another skillet of casserole dish, pour a small amount of sauce in the skillet then lay two egg wraps on top. I like to use an iron skillet the same size as the wraps. Spread half of the ground beef on top of the wraps. Then pour half of the jar of pasta sauce onto the beef and smooth out. Top with half of the mozzarella cheese. Add two more egg wraps and layer again with remaining beef, sauce and cheese. Bake in preheated 350 degree oven for about 30-35 minutes or until cheese and sauce are melted and bubbly.

Store in refrigerator for up to three days. Freeze for up to two months.

Sloppy Joes

PREP TIME: 5 MIN   COOK TIME: 25   SERVINGS: 4

INGREDIENTS

- 2 lbs ground beef
- 1/3 cup diced onion
- 1/3 cup diced green pepper
- 1/2 cup sugar free low carb ketchup
- 1 Tbsp tomato paste
- 1 Tbsp brown sweetener
- 1 tsp yellow mustard
- 3/4 tsp chili powder
- 1/2 tsp Worcestershire sauce
- 1/2 tsp salt
- 1/4 tsp black pepper
- 1/2 tsp Xanthan gum

METHOD

Melt butter or olive oil in a large skillet on the stove top. Saute onion and green pepper for a. minute then add ground beef. Break it up and. brown until cooked through. Drain excess grease.

Make the sauce by adding the remaining. ingredients together to make the sauce in a small saucepan.

Pour the sauce over the browned ground beef. Let simmer for 10-15 minutes on low. Serve over chaffles, (page 10) or low carb buns. This is great topped with my signature coleslaw, (page 25)

Serving Size: 1 cup
Carbs 5g
Fiber 1g
Protein 58g
Fat 37g
Calories 610

Cheesy Ranch Chicken

PREP TIME:10 MIN   COOK TIME: 40   SERVINGS: 3

INGREDIENTS

- 3 large chicken breast
- 4 oz softened cream cheese
- 2 tsp ranch seasoning
- 1 cup shredded colby jack cheese
- 3 slices bacon crumbled
- 2 cups frozen cauliflower or broccoli

Serving Size: One Piece
Plus 1/3 of Veggies
Carbs 8g
Fiber 2g
Protein 58g
Fat 34g
Calories 576

METHOD

Mix cream cheese, Ranch seasoning and 1/2 of the shredded cheese. Spread mixture onto each chicken breast, top with the remaining cheese. Sprinkle bacon on top of cheese.

Fill the pan around the chicken with thawed cauliflower. Drizzle broccoli with salt and olive oil. Cover with foil and bake at 375 for 20 minutes. Remove foil and bake an additional 15 minutes.

When finished, garnish with green onions.

Eggroll In A Bowl

PREP TIME: 10 MIN   COOK TIME: 25   SERVINGS: 4

INGREDIENTS

- 1-lb ground beef
- ¼ cup red onion, diced
- 1 tbsp sesame oil
- 1 tbsp rice vinegar
- 1 tsp salt
- 2 tsps minced fresh garlic
- 1 tsp ground ginger
- ¼ cup Tamari sauce
- 1 (14 ounce) bag coleslaw mix
- 2 green onions, thinly sliced
- Pepper to taste

METHOD

Brown ground beef along with onions in a large skillet on the stovetop. Add sesame oil, salt, garlic and ginger. Stir for about one minute. Add Tamari sauce, rice vinegar and coleslaw mix. Stir and cook until slaw is soft or desired texture. Top with green onions.

Serving Size: 1 cup
Carbs 8g
Fiber 3g
Protein 33g
Fat 16g
Calories 314

Chicken Crust Pizza

PREP TIME: 10 MIN	COOK TIME: 30	SERVINGS: 8 Slices

INGREDIENTS

- 1 lb ground chicken
- 1 cup grated parmesan cheese
- 1 egg
- 1 tsp salt

Crust Only

Serving Size: 1 Slice

Carbs 2g

Fiber 0g

Protein 18g

Fat 310g

Calories 170

METHOD

Preheat Oven to 425 degrees. Mix all ingredients together. Spread onto a parchment lined pizza pan. Bake crust for 8 minutes, then remove from oven. Add desired sauce and toppings. Return to oven for 12-15 minutes or until cheese is golden brown.

Taco Casserole

PREP TIME: 10 MIN   COOK TIME: 35   SERVINGS: 4

INGREDIENTS

- 2 pounds ground beef
- 1/2 cup onion, diced
- 2 cloves garlic, minced
- 2 Tbsp homemade taco seasoning (pg 20)
- 4 eggs
- 2 cups Mexican cheese, shredded
- Desired toppings, salsa, sour cream, green onions, black olives, lettuce, guacamole, etc.

METHOD

Preheat oven to 350. Saute onions in a large ovenproof skillet in butter for about a minute and then add garlic and ground beef. Chop and cook until beef is browned and cooked through. Drain excess grease and then add taco seasoning and 1/4 cup water. Let simmer for a couple of minutes. Crack eggs and whisk, then add half of the cheese to the eggs and stir. Pour over beef then top with remaining cheese. Bake for about 20-25 minutes until cheese is melted and bubbly. Scoop portions out on a plate and top with desired toppings.

Serving Size:
1 of 4 equal servings
Nutrition:
Carbs 7g
Fiber 1g
Protein 63g
Fat 62g
Calories 835

Creamy Tuscan Chicken

PREP TIME: 10 MIN   COOK TIME: 30 MIN   SERVINGS: 4

INGREDIENTS

- 1 tbsp butter
- 4 chicken breast
- 1 tsp salt
- 1/2 tsp pepper
- 2 cloves garlic, minced
- 1 teaspoon Italian seasoning
- 1 cup chicken broth
- 1/2 cup heavy cream
- 2 Tbsp sundried tomatoes, chopped into small bits
- 1/2 cup grated parmesan cheese
- 1 cup fresh spinach chopped
- 1/2 cup shredded parmesan cheese

Serving Size: one piece
Carbs 5g
Protein 44g
Fat 23g
Calories 399

METHOD

Preheat oven to 375 degrees. In a large ovenproof skillet, (I prefer to use an iron skillet) heat the butter. Season chicken breasts with salt and pepper. Once butter is melted, brown chicken on both sides (3-4 minutes per side). Transfer chicken to a plate.

Return skillet to medium heat. Add garlic and cook for 1 minute. Stir in heavy cream, Italian seasoning & chicken broth. Simmer for about 5 minutes, while stirring. Stir in sun dried tomatoes. spinach, grated parmesan cheese.

Return chicken to skillet and spoon sauce over the chicken breasts. Sprinkle with shredded parmesan cheese. Place in the oven, and bake until chicken is cooked through about 15 minutes or until it reaches 165F internal temperature.

Best Meatloaf

PREP TIME: 10 MIN   COOK TIME: 60   SERVINGS: 8

INGREDIENTS

- 2 lbs ground beef
- 1 cup grated Parmesan cheese
- 1 cup crushed pork rinds
- 2 eggs
- 1/2 cup diced onion
- 1 tsp garlic powder
- 1 tsp Salt
- 1/2 tsp pepper
- 8 slices of bacon

METHOD

Mix all ingredients, except Bacon, together. Press meat mixture into a loaf pan. Lay strips of bacon on top of the meatloaf. Place in 375 degree oven, check for doneness after 45 minutes. May take up to an hour.

Serving Size: one piece of 8
Carbs 1g
Fiber 0g
Protein 48g
Fat 35g
Calories 506

Big Mac Salad with Special Sauce

PREP TIME: 10 MIN   COOK TIME: 15   SERVINGS: 2

INGREDIENTS

Special Sauce:
- 1/4 cup mayonnaise
- 2 tsp dill relish
- 2 tsp yellow mustard
- 1 tsp sugar free ketchup
- 1 tsp white wine vinegar
- 1 tsp paprika
- 1 tsp onion powder
- 1 tsp garlic powder

Salad:
- 1 lb ground beef
- 4 slices American cheese
- 4 cups chopped iceberg lettuce
- 1/4 cup diced onion
- 1/2 cup dill pickle chips
- 1 tsp sesame seeds
- salt and pepper

METHOD

Make special sauce with the sauce ingredients and refrigerate. Make four hamburger patties, season with salt and pepper. Fry or grill burgers until desired doneness. Melt cheese on top of burgers. Divide lettuce between two plates and place two patties onto each bed of lettuce. Top with onions and pickles. Spread two tablespoons of sauce across burgers. Sprinkle sesame seeds over salad and enjoy!

Serving Size: Salad w/ two patties
Carbs 12g
Fiber 3g
Protein 71g
Fat 63g
Calories 900

46

Italian Stuffed Meatballs

PREP TIME: 10 MIN   COOK TIME: 20   SERVINGS: 12 Meatballs

INGREDIENTS

- 1 lb ground beef
- 2 tsp Italian seasoning
- 1 tsp garlic powder
- 1 tbsp minced onion
- 1 tbsp dried parsley
- 3 mozzarella string cheese sticks cut into 12 pcs
- 1 cup low carb marinara sauce

METHOD

Mix all ingredients together except for cheese. Form balls and place a square of cheese in the center of each meatball. Seal beef around cheese. Bake at 375 for 20 minutes. Remove from oven, top with sauce and grated parmesan cheese Bake for an additional 5 minutes to melt cheese.

These can be stored in the refrigerator for up to three days and frozen for up to two months.

Serving Size: one meatball
Carbs 2g
Fiber 0g
Protein 9g
Fat 8g
Calories 114

Swedish Meatballs

PREP TIME: 10 MIN   COOK TIME: 30   SERVINGS: 12 Meatballs

INGREDIENTS

- 2/3 pound ground beef
- 1/3 pound ground pork
- 1 teaspoon salt
- 1/2 teaspoon pepper
- 1/4 teaspoon nutmeg
- 1/4 teaspoon allspice
- 1/4 cup minced onion
- 1 egg
- 1/4 cup beef broth
- 1/4 cup crushed pork rinds
  Gravy:
- 1 teaspoon xanthan gum
- 2 cups beef broth
- 4 ounces sour cream
- salt and pepper to taste

Serving Size: one meatball
Carbs 1g
Protein 13g
Fat 9g
Calories 139

METHOD

Preheat oven to 350 F. Sauté onion in butter until translucent. Transfer onion to a large bowl and add meats, spices, egg, and pork rinds. Mix gently until combined.

Melt 1 tablespoon butter in a skillet, form meatballs and cook until outside are evenly browned. Meatballs will still be pink inside, transfer to a baking dish. Pour 1/4 cup of the broth into dish over meatballs, cover dish with foil, bake 30 minutes. Meanwhile, Gravy:

Turn meatball drippings in the skillet on medium heat pour broth into drippings, slowly whisk in xanthan gum. Simmer until thick, stirring regularly. Add salt and pepper to taste. Remove from heat and stir in sour cream and pour over meatballs just before serving.

These can be stored in the refrigerator for up to four days and frozen for up to two months.

Chicken Cordon Bleu

PREP TIME: 10 MIN   COOK TIME: 30   SERVINGS: 2

INGREDIENTS

- 2 large chicken breasts
- Salt & pepper to taste
- 4 slices prosciutto
- 4 slices Swiss cheese
- 4 slices bacon

Serving Size: one piece
Carbs 1g
Fiber 0g
Protein 77g
Fat 32g
Calories 538

METHOD

Pound chicken breast flat between parchment paper using a meat tenderizer. Salt and pepper both sides. Layer prosciutto and cheese on top of each piece of chicken. Roll chicken up and wrap with bacon. Each piece may need two strips of bacon. Secure with toothpicks.

Bake 350 degrees 24-28 minutes or 165 internal temperature.

Green Bean Stroganoff

PREP TIME: 10 MIN   COOK TIME: 30   SERVINGS: 4

INGREDIENTS

- 1 pound ground beef
- 4 slices of bacon chopped into small pieces
- 1/2 cup onion diced
- 1 clove garlic minced
- 1/2 cup fresh sliced mushrooms
- 1 tsp xanthan gum (thickener)
- 2 cups beef broth
- 2 teaspoons Worcestershire sauce
- salt & pepper to taste
- 1/2 cup sour cream
- 2 cups frozen green beans
- 1 cup shredded parmesan cheese
- 1 tablespoon dried parsley

METHOD

Brown ground beef, bacon, onion and garlic. Drain fat. Add mushrooms and cook for 3 minutes. Add broth, Worcestershire sauce, salt, pepper and sprinkle xanthan gum across the top of the liquid. Bring to a boil. While stirring, reduce heat and simmer on low 10 minutes. Add green beans and heat through. Turn off heat, stir in sour cream and parsley. Top with parmesan. cheese and let melt, serve.

Serving Size: 1 serving of 4
Carbs 10g
Fiber 2g
Protein 45g
Fat 35g
Calories 536

Air Fryer Breaded Shrimp

PREP TIME: 10 MIN   COOK TIME: 15   SERVINGS: 4

INGREDIENTS

- 1 pound large shrimp (16/20 count), peeled and deveined, tails on
- 1 tsp Old Bay Seasoning
- 1 cup pork panko (crushed pork rinds)
- 2 eggs, beaten
- 1/2 cup grated parmesan cheese
- Cooking Spray

Serving Size: 5-6 Shrimp
Carbs 1g
Fiber 0g
Protein 70g
Fat 25g
Calories 505

METHOD

Pat thawed shrimp dry between a couple of paper towels. Whisk pork panko, parmesan cheese and Old Bay seasoning together in a shallow dish. Whisk the eggs in a shallow bowl. Dip shrimp one by one into the beaten eggs. Dredge in the crumb mixture turning until evenly coated. Transfer to air fryer and repeat with the remaining shrimp. Preheat air fryer to 385 degrees F. Place the shrimp in a single layer in the fryer basket, then spray lightly with cooking spray. Cook, flipping halfway through, until the shrimp are golden brown and cooked through, about 10-12 minutes.

Chicken Enchilada Casserole

PREP TIME: 10 MIN   COOK TIME: 15   SERVINGS: 6

INGREDIENTS

- 3 cups shredded rotisserie chicken
- 4 Crepini Egg Wraps
- 2 Tbsp taco seasoning (pg 21)
- 2 cans 10 oz Enchilada Sauce
- 12 oz Muenster Cheese
- Sour Cream for Topping

METHOD

Start by spreading a couple of tablespoons of enchilada sauce on the bottom of an oven safe skillet. Layer two ply wraps, 1/2 of the chicken, 1/2 of the sauce and 1/2 of the cheese. Top with 2 more wraps, the remaining chicken, sauce and cheese. Bake 375 degrees for 25-30 minutes or until cheese is brown and bubbly. Top with sour cream.

Serving Size: 1/6 piece
Carbs 8g
Fiber 1g
Protein 24g
Fat 17g
Calories 294

CHAPTER 6
DESSERT

"Let food be thy medicine & medicine be thy food"

Cannoli Dip

PREP TIME: 10 MIN   SERVINGS: 24

INGREDIENTS

- 16 oz Ricotta cheese
- 8 oz mascarpone cheese
- 1 tsp vanilla extract
- 1/2 cup powdered sweetener
- chocolate chips (optional)
- pistachios (optional)

METHOD

Add ricotta and mascarpone to a mixing bowl and beat with mixer until combined. Add vanilla and sweetener and beat until light and fluffy. Top with chopped pistachio or chocolate chips. Refrigerate for up to four days. Serve with Pizzelle (Recipe page 55)

(I do not count carbs in sweeteners, if you do, you need to refigure the carb count)

Serving Size: two tablespoons
Carbs 1g
Fiber 0g
Protein 2g
Fat 7g
Calories 68

Pizzelle

PREP TIME: 10 MIN   COOK TIME: 60   SERVINGS: 20 Pizzelle

INGREDIENTS

- 4 eggs
- ⅔ cup Monkfruit granulated sweetener
- 1 tsp extract of choice (anise, almond, or vanilla)
- ½ cup butter, melted
- 2 cups almond flour
- ½ tsp baking powder
- ¼ teaspoon salt

METHOD

Mix all ingredients together with an electric mixer. Scoop a tablespoon at a time into Pizzelle Maker. They only take about two minutes. Let cool on cooling rack. They will be pliable until cool then they will crisp up. You can mold them while they are warm into cones or mini bowls.

(I do not count carbs in sweeteners, if you do, you need to refigure the carb count)

Serving Size: one
Carbs 2g
Fiber 1g
Protein 3g
Fat 10g
Calories 108

Paula's Signature Ice Cream

PREP TIME: 10 MIN   SERVINGS: 6

INGREDIENTS

- 1-1/2 Cup heavy cream
- 1-1/2 Cup almond milk unsweetened
- 1 tsp vanilla extract
- 3/4 cup Allulose

Serving Size: 1/2 cup
Carbs 4g
Fiber 0g
Protein 4g
Fat 44g
Calories 424

METHOD

Whisk all ingredients in a bowl until allulose is dissolved. Add to an electric ice cream maker. Follow directions on ice cream maker. Allulose is a very important ingredient in this ice cream. It keeps the ice cream soft and scoopable even after freezing. You may also use unsweetened coconut milk in place of heavy cream for a dairy free option.

Store in an airtight container in the freezer.

(I do not count carbs in sweeteners, if you do, you need to refigure the carb count)

Easy Peanut Butter Fudge

PREP TIME: 10 MIN   SERVINGS: 12

INGREDIENTS

- 1 cup no sugar added peanut butter (ground peanuts)
- 1 stick butter
- 3/4 cup powdered sweetener 1
- tsp vanilla extract
- 1/2 tsp Salt

Serving Size: one piece
Carbs 2g
Fiber 1g
Protein 4g
Fat 15g
Calories 157

METHOD

Line an 8-inch square baking pan with parchment paper.
Add the peanut butter and butter to a medium mixing bowl. Cover the bowl and microwave for a minute at a time, until the butter is melted. Remove the bowl from the microwave and add the vanilla and salt. Stir until the mixture is well combined.
Add the sugar-free powdered sweetener and stir until combined. Pour into pan and place in refrigerator for 4-6 hours.
Cut into squares.
Store in refrigerator.

(Make sure your sweetener of choice is Keto approved. I do not count carbs in sweeteners, if you do, you need to refigure the carb count)

Made in United States
North Haven, CT
04 May 2024

52101674R00033